# WITHIN SHADES OF
# MAHOGANI

## KAY JACOBS

authorHOUSE®

*AuthorHouse™*
*1663 Liberty Drive*
*Bloomington, IN 47403*
*www.authorhouse.com*
*Phone: 1 (800) 839-8640*

*Published by AuthorHouse 01/03/2018*

*ISBN: 978-1-5462-1946-0 (sc)*
*ISBN: 978-1-5462-1944-6 (hc)*
*ISBN: 978-1-5462-1945-3 (e)*

*Library of Congress Control Number: 2017918510*

*Print information available on the last page.*

I dedicate
this book to
the many muses
that made me feel like
I had no voice;
because of you,
I screamed my thoughts
onto these pages…
Thank You.

# Acknowledgements:

To my English Language Arts/Reading & Writing teachers:

Mrs. Helen Cannon, Ms. T-Rose (pre-school), Ms. Deborah Cato & Ms. Boyd (Head Start), Mrs. Sue Triche, Ms. Barbara Smith (lower elementary), Mrs. Patricia Gomez, Ms. Stephanie Washington-Williams (upper elementary), Mrs. Ann Buisson, Mrs. Carmen Johnson, Mrs. Barbara Forshag, Mrs. Billie Bumgarner (middle school), Mrs. Judith Field, Mr. Joseph Binet, Ms. Rebecca Bordelon, Mrs. Jeri Landry (high school), Dr. Kris Lackey, and Dr. Kay Murphy (undergraduate): these individuals tirelessly gave of themselves in preparing me for this moment of my existence - many thanks.

To my family and friends: Twiggy & Jake, the class of 1997's Get Fresh Crew, my family Flossy posse', and the many members of my XULA family - thank you for your support.

To Kendra Fiffie-Williams, Elgin Pierre, 'Dr' Jermaine Zanders, and Rev. Rodney Johnson – special thanks to you for your unwavering motivation.

To my impenetrable, God-stained Rock and two precious Pebbles: I will always love you three forever.

# Contents

# iConnect:

When Nature has work to be done, she creates a genius to do it.
Ralph Waldo Emerson

# Love Poem No. 2

(inspired by *The Bodyguard* soundtrack)

deeply awaiting
the beat to relax
the temperate being
dwelling within

trumpet slowly,
softly blowing
a cautious wind through
my humbled, lonely soul

piano playing in the
darkness of mine heart
chipping away at
its emptiness

and the only thing
left to ponder is the fact
that I've lost
my bodyguard

where are you,
my love?

bright white clouds
in the spacious light, blue sky;
freedom consuming
the natural herbs of life

grey lake's waters
crashing against each other
in the mysterious
glow of gravity

sun taking a peak
to look at me – down on me
as if it were scolding me
for what I'd done

yet, the graceful song
still continues to play
in the corners of my serene,
solemn realm.

For my bodyguard, my love,
Is lost.

# Twinkle, twinkle, my greatest love

the sun's reflection
gleamed on a rippled lake
putting me into a deep trance
of emotional confusion
delighted as the largest star stole
its guiding light from the earth
to end yet another rotation on a tilted
axis
intrigued by the water's waves
as they began to arise
and drench the green-clad
stone steps of the shore
mystified by a beautiful horizon
complimenting the luxurious sunset
as a soft, calm blow from God
caressed the back of my neck
appreciative of nature in its
perfect state of peace and tranquility
surprised by the quacks
that startled this flow
and by the cracks of the leaves
beneath a pair of spherical feet
disturbed by the brakes
and whistles of modern-day Model T's
as the world turns and
speeds our lives on their ways
I wondered upon an unseen star
where you are
and if you were thinking of me

# MY GETAWAY

UNLIMITED CLEAR BLUENESS
ACCENTUATED WITH A
STREAKING TANGERINE RAY
COMPLEMENTING A PEACEFUL DAY'S END
TO INTRODUCE A SECOND OF KNOWN
QUIET NIGHTS TO ME

PROXIMITY IS NOT ESSENTIAL –
NO CARS' BUSY BUSTLE TO WORK
NO NEIGHBORS FOR MILES AROUND
WIDE OPEN COUNTRYSIDE
OF ROLLING GREEN FLATLANDS
STRETCHING AS FAR AS ETERNITY
FULL OF NATURE AT ITS HIGEST PEAK
OAKS, ELMS, AND PINES
REACHING TO TOUCH HEAVEN'S GATES
AS WINGED SINGERS CHIRP
THEIR MELODIOUS SONGS OF SERENITY
THE MOST CRISP AIR
MY NOSE HAD EVER TASTED
COOL BREEZES OF TRANQUILITY
RIPPLING UPON THE WATERS OF THE FRONT YARD POND

I SIT ON ITS BANK
AND AM CONSUMED –
MIND, BODY, SOUL
THAT FAMILIAR NEGATIVE ESSENCE OF HOME
INSTANTLY DESTROYED
FOR THIS SIMPLE HERMITAGE TO SOME
FEELS LIKE A TOTAL PARADISE –
AS IF IT ONLY EXISTS
JUST FOR ME
TO BE FREE

RE: AMITE, LA

# before and after

Raindrops falling on the
grass growing on the
lawn chair where the birds
built their nest
egg for april who starts
college next fall

Sun peeking through the
clouds shaped like fig
trees in full blossom
'cause summer smells so sweet

Children playing hop
scotch on uncle willie's breath
of cool air sweeping
over the barbeque pit
bull chasing after the neighborhood alley
cat that sits on the side
of the ditch eating sugarcane and grape huckabucks
'cause summer tasted so sweet

Perched on a branch of the Great Pecan
pie that Gram's baking in the kitchen
sink full of dirty sunday dinner dishes

I cannot take it all in

but while pondering upon all that's now lost
the wind slaps a bouquet of dandelions into the air
spewing its pollen
tickling my nostrils
caressing my face
so I made a wish and
summer never felt sweeter…

A-choo!

# Your face

Deep beneath the sheets I lay;
    Snuggled close to me, my baby doll.
A crack in my curtain, a peek in my window
    I see your face so clear.
Your pale white color, your shining light
    Brings security and comfort
    All through the dark night.

# Breathe Again

Look into the eyes of sorrow
and find a river of strength
flowing deep within your soul;
Follow the path less taken
to a wondrous field of dreams,
untouched by the living and the dead
but rather filled by one's imagination
creating mysteries and realms unchartered –
catching you by surprise
and leaving you breathless.

Sit upon the wings of love
and journey to captivating places
discovering new life and new civilizations;
express an sense of inner being
overcome with endless excitement,
yet, distracted by the hands of time
slowly bringing you back to reality:
loud noise and much disturbance,
ignorance and destruction plaguing the land –
still leaving you breathless.

# A Simple Day

Kissed the rain
Slammed the door
Yelled the snow
Swept the floor
Sang the sky
Flickered the light
Spanked the sea
Flew a kite
Smiled the sun
Rang the phone
Slapped the wind
Ate a cone
Cried the shore
Washed the clothes
Frowned the clouds
Took a doze

# When the Wind Blows

*When the wind blows, I hear music –*
*Sweet and soft as a baby's skin.*
*When the wind blows, I feel warmth*
*As if sitting by a slightly lit fire.*
*When the wind blows, I get scared;*
*Thinking something bad will happen next.*
*When the wind blows, it soothes my soul*
*And a feeling of comfort comes over me.*
*When the wind blows, I feel sudden changes,*
*Feelings so deep, I just can't explain.*


1993

# Lullaby of a Lonely Heart

Wind sang its sweet song
　　of lonely sorrow last night
Seas danced that which
　　is forbidden alone yesterday
Cried my first tears of joy
　　at your disenchanting appearance
So that you may continue
　　your life without me everyday

Wind whispered soft somethings
　　in my weary ear as
　　the seas laughed loudly
　　and the trees applauded
　　　　heartbroken defeat
I smiled spitefully
to calm my nerves and
subdue my thoughts
to withstand yet another agenda
　　of betrayal
But, I stand tall
　　like the woman that I am
　　and fear what the refrain
　　of this wretched song will bring

# delirium on Monday nights

i am a bird.
you are a flea.
i pick you off of my wing,
and put you in my drink.
you swim wildly;
you gasp for air.
you climb the side of the glass,
and you die right there.
as my lips approach to sip,
i look into your eyes and think
your guts taste good as
they drip down my chin
and into the sink.

# never again

A misty cloud
left behind by the dust
of Love's ashes
was blown away by
a calm wind
created by the axial rotation
of a full indigo moon.
She looked upon its face,
turned away solemnly,
and bade Love
goodbye
for a final time.

# from Dusk until Dawn

glistening dewdrops whisper,
telling me to wait
until Day closes its eyes
to behold the arrival of its
better half;

shy Moon hides behind
the shiny twinkles of fluorescence
as they decorate
a glorious background
of un-reflected light
ending the Sun's reign;

glorifying the evolution of Nature –
illuminating the nature of Existence –
disguising my existence in Life.

# Hot Bath After Work

Incenses burn sensuously floating
white streams of thin steam into the atmosphere
as I meditate in the relaxing waves of foam that embodies me.

# TIME STOPPED AS I TURNED TO SEE

WHAT THE END WOULD BRING
THROUGH THE DOORS OF THIS REALITY
THAT SEEMS SO ENDLESS TO UNPREDICTABILITY.
THE RED LIGHT TURNED GREEN
SIMULTANEOUSLY AS I WALKED ACROSS
LIFE'S TREACHEROUS PATHWAY.
THEN, AFTER THE RAIN
FINALLY CEASED TO EXIST FLOATING
AGAINST THE ORANGE HORIZONED SKY,
I SAW THE SILVER LINING BEHIND THE CLOUD-
SUPPOSEDLY THAT POSITIVE ASPECT
OF ANY NEGATIVE SITUATIONS THAT IS HANDED ON
ONE'S PLATTER
THE TWINKLE IN THE TWILIGHT
INTRODUCING THE PREMIERE OF A FULL MOON
WISHED UPON AND MESMORIZED NONETHELESS
GAVE A SENSE OF HOPE DESPITE DESPAIR
AND ANGUISH
I BLINKED…I RUBBED MY EYES…
AND AWAKENED TO BEHOLD MY ONE TRUE LUST
IN LIFE
A LACK OF COMPANIONSIP, A LOST OF WORDS
AND THE ONLY THING THAT COULD SET MY SOUL FREE –
SECURITY THAT ENSURED MY FREEDOM AND
INDEPENDENCE

THEN, I EXHALED…


1999

# I LOOK TO YOU...

When you're down to nothing, God is up to something...

# I'm Missing You

It's morning
and I restlessly slept the night away.
I cried myself to sleep
as the moon supplied the warmth
of your comforting caress last night –
and for the nearing lonely nights to
come,
I will forever miss your face
gracing me as the sun does now
to introduce a brand new day.
You were my sunshine,
but you are no longer here to brighten
my gloomy days –
at least, not in this lifetime.
You will never again receive my
wake-up calls.
I will never embrace you in my arms
or will we ever enjoy each other's
company:
our times of pure bliss and joy,
our proclamations of love
in this mortality.
But since I know
that everything happens for a reason
and God has a reason for everything
that happens,
I await your sweet, eternal touch
until the dawning of a different day;
in a newness of life
where we will never part ever again.

For in this moment of time
that I have shared with you
in precious harmony,
I realized exactly how much

you still mean to me.
So, finally
when the Heaven-bound
effervescence of light
should shine upon me,
I'll meet you in God's eternity
to spend all of my life
with you once again.

Oh –
If I could just see you
one more morning
when I open my eyes.
*Good night, my Darling.*


*From the front desk of Bienville Hall –
for Ms. Octavia*

# No Peace within the Sanctuary

you make it hard for me to love you
you make it hard for me to leave
but to your empty words, I can no longer cleave

in your presence, you disgust me
in your absence, I'm depressed
there is no direct line where this ends in happyness

yet you are loved as I am too
but if she was here…

it was a strong connection;
people saw it the first day. And
when she smiled at you,
like all others, your heart you gave away.

She would have been so happy
She would have made you proud
Because her essence lightened the darkest of days
Creating many silver-lined clouds

Yet now all that remains
Is me trying not to go insane
Wrenching, a troubled wretch in pain
At the thought of this triangle
That is being maintained

Even with her angelic soul –
Her torment – finally lain to rest
Deep down
We both - all, know
She will always be your very best.

And I - no one, can compete with that.

# f.y: I.D.

(for you: I. Dee)

shy at when first I laid eyes on you
scared to simply say hello
enchanted by your accessorized visage
enticed by your smooth, sensitive smile
bewildered by your muscular frame

I wanted to just talk to you for awhile

curious about future conversations
hopes for more personal relations
fears due to other temptations
anxiously awaiting any social engagements
your gentle touch sending multiple vibrations

glad I was able to talk to you for awhile

the sweet caress of your kiss
quality time of purely platonic bliss
emotions running wild and free
maybe it all happened a bit too quickly
but friends forever were we only meant to be

thanks for the chance to talk to you…for a while


(RIP 1999)

# A Daughter's Plea

the **C**aring thoughts that were hoped for
the **O**nly person who could have shared
the **M**any ways I felt neglected
the **P**romises broken every time they were made
the **R**espect that was never given
the **O**ther 'issues' always involved
the **M**illions of tears that have been shed
the **I**gnorance always shown
the **S**ilence that quiets my thoughts
the **E**verlasting, overbearing control

You were an undeniable strain on my life,
A never-ending point of stress and strife;
Through time and space, we have finally found
    the median of our relationship -
even though we are not joined at the hip,
we are stronger than we've ever been
and that's all the compromise I've ever needed it!

# Love Jones' Stories #9: Remorse

I guess I'll never work up enough nerve to tell you
how much sometimes I miss you.
Despite the animosity between us,
there was something about being with you
that made the difference.
The way we would go out to the movies
or just eating out
(even though someone else paid for it)
had its value to me.
And no matter how much we fussed
and argued over simple, petty shit,
we would-we could always laugh after it.
As funny and unbelievable as this may seem,
I miss that about you.
Sure you had your secrets
(shit that devastated me no doubt),
but who doesn't.
And I'm not taking your side or
letting that shit slide;
Right now, for some odd reason,
I wish you were here –
If not to take me out,
Just to make me laugh after some stupid argument –
Help me to feel like something…
Someone who matters to somebody;
I just wish you were here
Right Now.

*26   octobre   99*

# nina moseley

it's been days since last we spoke
as the memories of us rush
    my mental horizons
flooding my mind with pictures of love
flushing out the drive to move on –

yet, I know that I must!
I guess I just needed to know
    That you are okay

So I called you *67
Just to hear your voice say
Hello.

# Everything Happens for a Reason

There's a deep silence all around;
    A sound that has even muffled the loudest mouths.
There's a remorseful regret –
    Something that's keeping the silence alive;
    A hope for life…a fear of sudden death.

No one is promised tomorrow, but
    No one has knowledge about today, and
Everything happens for a reason, they say.

I guess that He, the Almighty, has a plan;
    Whether good or bad, sooner or later – the Grimmest Pain comes.
I guess it has nothing to do with morals
    Because they were perfect and pure;
    Still Death came knocking at their doors.
It came within the blink of the eye;
    It came without anyone knowing why, yet
    Everything happens for a reason, they say.

It's too late to bring them back-
    Those three who were so loved
    And so cherished dearly.
It's too late to ask why –
    Their tomorrow will never come
and their today is gone forever.
There's nothing that can be said or done
    For their eternal battle has been won;
    Still –
    Everything happened for a reason, they say.

*In dedication to Sherry, Jamie, and Stacey 1996*

# Simple Liberation and the Possibility of Faith Nevermore

Good Morning, Langston –

it ain't been no crystal stare,
my life that is;
and I, too, Sing America
despite my Deferred Dreams –
throughout all of the Boogies
as Simple as it may seem;
I've also known rivers.
I've given Fine Clothes to the Jew
on a one-way ticket
to hear Shakespeare in Harlem;
still, you hear me singing
The Weary Blues.

Good afternoon, Emily –

if I can stop one heart from beating
because I could not stop for death,
I could then dwell in possibility.
I've tasted a liquor never brewed;
I've seen a dying eye
in the bustle of a house
where lightning was a yellow fork
lighted by a yellow star
in wild nights of Heaven –
the one thing I cannot reach.
after great pain, a formal feeling
came called Faith – a fine invention.

Good Evening, Nikki –

Nikki-rosa told me
to tell you that.
lately, I've been having Revolutionary
Dreams
of Black Talk and Black Judgment
re:creating the true import of our
present
dialogue while Ego-tripping.
I've spun a soft black song of
Liberation
as I observed the women and the
men –
Those who ride the night wind
eating cotton candy on a rainy day
during vacation time
in front of my house.

Good Night, Edgar –

I find it funny that
Death has reared himself a throne
in my life, but
it is to Helen that I write
many and many a year ago
from that Kingdom by the sea,
where the melancholy waters lie
over the moon
down to the valley of the shadow;
how like a statue I stand tall,
quoth the Raven nevermore.

# this spiritual thang

good morning, sunshine -
glad to see you slept well last night.
I watched you for a while
in your deep state of dreamin'
before falling fast asleep beside you.
as we laid together in spooning
position,
I felt a little poke come from you.
instinct told me how to react
for it had been much too long
since you honored me with
that such greeting of anxious
excitement.
I rolled over on my side to face you,
kissed you on the cheek,
your eyes failed to meet mine
halfway
but still I continued on this
expedition.
to entice you, I massaged your body
orally;
I resurfaced from the love below
to finally have our eyes aligned
meeting a place beyond Eden's
satisfaction
the sheer sex in your eyes
hypnotized me
causing me to lose my sense of self
in our pure innocence
like this was our first time.
you reached deep into my soul
spewing words I had never heard
before
I surrendered to your whims,

intertwined within the satin of your
sheets
before the sun said hello to begin
another seven score less than eternity
with you
you smiled; I swept the single tear
of bliss
from the left side of my face and
returned to the comfort of your
embrace
finally, the happiness we both
deserved
and I enjoyed every spiritual moment
of this thang-
throughout the darkest, most fretful
storms to
the gladdest shores of security
for an eternal fortnight
under every full moon
that shines its light of love
that guided us to each other.
This love we share
stands the tests of time
and in this such factor,
everything will be reborn.

# Miss U Not

(Upon hearing of your departure to San Diego,
good luck in your future endeavors)

I thought of you today
while sipping sweet tea
I thought I saw you for a minute
there
standing tall with arms wide open
to embrace me
A re-union of proportions
unexplainable
and I looked into the dark brown
of your eyes
as you looked into mine
and you smirked
and I cringed
as you slyly slithered back
into my spiritual garden
watering that planted see
I thought had died.

But as I looked
over your shoulder –
still, the steadfast soldier you were-
my eyes beheld

a blossomed bud
a new garden
sprouting spores of
life and love;
this seed developing
from that universally strange thing
at first sight
in addition to
a friendship…
something we never could seem
to establish
so just between you and me
that weed that grew
so lustfully
is finally exterminated;

but it was good seeing you again
even if only in a dream,
our reality remains supreme
and it is over.

# What You See Through my God and me

As I fell to my knees
I begged the Lord to forgive me please
For I have sinned against thee…
You see –
When I first laid eyes on you
I knew I had to make you my boo
I felt you were something to be pursued
You see –
Although you rejected to be mine
I respected that, thought that was fine
For to see my inner beauty would mean for you to be blind
You see –
I asked thou for forgiveness,
Mind you it's none of your business
But I just had to be a true witness
To the fact that you're only a tease
Just like untouched honey to a swarm of bees
Yet, you have crossed my unchartered seas
You see –
Unfortunately, to love me is to hate me
And to want me, you must acquire the money to provide me my desires;
Let me interpret the truth behind
The simple complexities of my tampered mind
For my body stands innocent and kind
You see –
It's my soul that needs to be made whole
Despite my urgent demand for control
You are the potter, I am the clay you would want to mold
You see.

# At Last, She's Free

When your life is the whirlwind before the storm
and you have to successfully live it

When your creativity is stifled, overshadowed by the
desires of the mainstream for the love of money

When one's in love so bad, so hard, so deep that rage and
jealousy rear their heads of destruction (by way of fire)

When thug style met a female wild with a lyrical tongue
to appeal to the youth of a confused generation

When sexy and cool teamed up with crazy to respond to their fan
mail after filing for bankruptcy despite their platinum status

When the public eye only sees you and the embodiment
emotional insanity and uncontrollable instability

When the inner peace consumes you and you're re-established
into the realm of normalcy, acknowledged by the Almighty

When changes from one's wicked ways to walking in
a more glorious light becomes your daily walk

That's when life comes to its end; Life continues
to exist, just not within you any longer;
For He's satisfied with your decisions and you have completed your journey.

That's when and I believe that's why
She was the one that, on that day, died.


RIP Lisa "left eye" Lopes
04.25.02


29

# I STILL YEARN FOR FREEDOM

*"In a world that is sick with —isms, get well soon."* Janet Jackson

# sexuality

something as simple as
that which distinguishes you
from the next in line

everything that completes
your individuality should
never be considered benign

anything so sacrificial
you hide it in a closet
to release sometime after nine

all those things which make you
unique, true, and eccentric
one of a kind

nothing than a distortion
of self, a symbol indeed
one needs not know mine

# DESIRE

I need you to go away
I need you to leave my space
I need you to stop your lies
I need you to say good-bye

I need this feeling to stray
I needed your words not to stay
I needed you to hardcore tweak
I needed you to get downright weak

I need me to be whole again
Even if that means not having you as a friend
I need you to go away
This I pray,
Amen.

# Murderer

(another teenager destroying her life...)
Com'on baby
Gurl, clam down
You won't feel a thang
(my lucky day – a virgin!)
Just relax
I'll take good care of you
'cause you my lady
(I gotta this b**** some morning after pills)
Boo, you know – of course
I love you – right
I would never make you do nuthin'
you don't wanna do
I'll never do nuthin' to hurt you
Com'on lemme 'come' inside
No, trust me
It's better natural
(a jimmie?? like I got some shyt!)
Don't be scared
There ain't nuthin' to be nervous about
(man, she betta let me hit -
it's been 2 ½ weeks; I've been patient, hell!!)
I promise
I'll take good care of you...aight...
If you relax, you won't even feel it –

(another teenager trying to save her life)
Calm down, baby girl
Take a couple of deep breaths
I know this is your first
(and hopefully your last until you're ready)
and I'm going to do everything I can
to make you as comfortable as possible
because you remind me of my own
(I better suggest the pill)
Yes, I know
He said he loved you
Yes, it's okay
I'm taking care of you...we're taking care of it
now – okay
I need you to put your feet here
Scoot your body all the way down
Open your legs as wide as you can
Relax your muscles
Don't be scared
You're doing great
You're going to feel a little stick
Calm down – I know you're scared
Take a deep breath...
Ready...(sounds of a vacuum cleaner)...
You didn't even feel a thing.

# -The Now Generation –

(1994)

let us live our lives as we wish and as we want.
we're not so say rebelling by getting pregnant
or into a gang. we're only asking for lives
that we're satisfied with and can enjoy.
we're not slaves or maids or servants
or babies not adults. we are adoles-
cents and sort of demand a lil'
Respect to live as past
generations have
done. don't
treat us like
outcasts but don't
cage us like animals
or keep us from living –
attitudes come with
the territory of
our lives and
we want
Freedom!

# pipe dreams

designer clothes
money, cash, whores,
living lavish at your own mode of
comfort
shopping sprees
high tech schemes
spending excessively
for you own personal trends and
styles
you and your
pipe dreams
running wild
expensive cars
family wars
telling lies as fast as a horse can trot
your new philosophy
complimenting
your better life
filled with
flossing and bossing
controller – big money grip roller
you and your
pipe dreams
running wild
crazy friends
drinking gin
smoking that herb
continuously, never-ending
never mind the fact
that the cops are on your back
trying to catch you in the act
showcasing your new roofed
possessions
billiards table
big screens and flat tvs

hot tubs and jacuzzis
swimming pool
marble stoned – inner and out
three piece loveseat
laced curtains and silky satin sheets
all of life's finer luxuries
even a chandelier
absorbing the heat of
you and your
pipe dreams
running wild
no more sharing
care less about caring
constantly bearing
those innumerable funds
indignantly left to you
the dollar signs in your eyes
said this was a deadly surprise
I knew it would be trouble
you changed quickly
personality three times over doubled
all psyched up to take
a hard fall due to
you and your
pipe dreams
running wild
so
whenever the depressions
should kick into high gear
and you just happen
to shed some grievingly painful tears
your world torn apart
your identity abducted
your mentality misconstrued
your cipher abruptly stopped

due to an abundance
of high hopes afloat
and big dreams of esteem and wealth
that overpowered your asinine drive
for life
you'll be left standing alone
a motionless, hopeless
shell of a man – of you
a lil' penniless, pitiful frame of being
with the hole in your heart
and the shallowness of your
soul's remains
deteriorating you from
the inside out
you and your
pipe dreams
that ran wild and free
excluding everyone
that should have held
Value to you
Your offspring
Your brethren
The one you proclaimed
The love of your life
I hope…
you'll enjoy
yourself
with your life of
pipe dreams
blowing in the wind
that imaginative
very dim
and narrow
aspect
of
your
reality

(1999)

# Stepping Out of Your Life with a Little Room to Breathe

(2000, revised 2015)

I can't seem to release myself
from those who
mentally betray me –
that socially persecute me
because of my desire
to live my life right.

With my back shoved up
in a corner of disarray,
I search through my soul's
debris to find a sense
of acceptance.

What is this that depresses me
so to a point of unknowingness?
Why do they – why does it
internally torture me so badly…
why can't I overcome it? them?

There is no longer
a sense of self-worth;
self-confidence left this realm
before it could be born
into importance.

I try so hard to be
someone I'm not,
so that you could be proud of me-
But in your eyes,
I've done nothing
more than breathe … but no more!

I want to be free
to be me and be accepted
for who I am;
not look in the mirror
and see all of the belittlement
I've endured.

If you choose to scorn me
for 'disobedience' –
not following your agenda
to succumb to failure,
so be it…

Just be reminded:
I am not you
so don't punish me
for the mistakes you've made
in your past
hindering my present
erasing our future.

I respect you more than that.
I've loved you in spite of.
I will transform
your selfish ways
into the climax of my life.

It is no longer what you want for me
but rather, what I need to do for
myself…
All I ask is that you don't make me
choose –

the continuance of optimism that
drives my life versus
the continuous end of my sanitybecause
I will choose Me over
you now
Every time.

# P.S. 2158 (Political Science)

bang!
the shot that rang
through the large crowd
of people
shouting praises to the man who
would bring
them to the brinks of
equality
and peace of mind
for those who were
oppressed
by the white
authority
on a power trip
because the government gave them
control
to brutalize
an already battered
race of people
scarred by slavery
physically bruised, beaten
mentally bruised, inferior
to an ignorant race
of dominance
because of the
color
of their skin
so respected as
pure
versus the
ethnicity
of ebony
bronzes

searching, looking, wandering
for a way out
of their unfortunate
situation –
their living conditions
due to an
evident,
unequally separate
intentional
lack of education
of opportunity
of reason
of choice
of knowledge
now presented in
various symbols of
inner peace
introspections of the
tormented souls
of a
greatly influential people
that brought
dance to a new height
strived to gain
their civil rights
just to be
rightfully revered as
individuals
first-class
citizens
of this melting pot
desiring consolation
for the past

actions
endured against them – Us.
and as that leader
of the congregation
speaking about
change
and revolutionary
Revelations
without militancy and violence
laid there
on the
green
earth
red
stiff, unmovable
in the
blackness
of death
a sorrowful voice
whispers
through the crowd
demandingly asking
can't we all just get along
erase racism
and live in unity
power to All our people
across this
Earth
and
just
for once
be
Free?

# Prelude to the Millennium

It has been written
in the Great Book of Guidance for Life
that He would destroy this world
yet for a second time;
a world riddled with chaos and destruction
by way of an inflamed thunder
of orange bursts
like that of the Eternal Underworld.
That, we have not yet seen;
But what this world is experiencing its termination:
tamed canines killing sheer innocence
keenly constructed aircrafts having unsuccessful flights
inner rages and outer battles contaminating
    the physicality of countries
threats to the international economy due to
    fear of technological shutdown
intellectual individuals holding co-workers hostage
students on mental rampages causing
    emotionally fatal situations
modes of ground transportation's destinations
    being deadly collisions
defacing of national identities
reconstructing the next generation's youth
internal wars of self damnation;
replanting the roots of a civilized society
in an effort to secure
    this world's existence
    this continent's welfare
    this country's reputation
    this state's legislative prosperity
    this area's economic status
    this school's value of education
    this class's social integrity –
This poem has been dedicated
to realizing the effects of an exalted crisis;

The world is coming to its end,
The countdown has begun
5
4
3
2...

# MERCY, MERCY ME

what is going on
around here
inside my head
racing through
my mind
consuming my thoughts
empty, shallow, bitter
images surrounding
the central of
my cipher
my life
turning
upside down
in a whirlwind
of confusion
leaving me
bewildered
at this consistent
state of dumbfoundedness
truly plaguing
my conscience
with remorseful
regret and guilt
and sorrow and
loneliness

what is going on
around here
inside my heart
feelings tainted
by disillusions
of imperfections
pictures of
lovers in love
holding hands
expressing emotions
beyond their own
little imaginations
once friends
now almost foes
tension so thick
one can deeply
gage it with a knife
straight through
my world
of discontent

what is going on
around here
inside the realms
of my so-called life

# Love Jones' Stories: End Saga

I cried in the shower
so that no one could see
the single tear
walk down alongside my face
because it was over...

you no longer care and
I have lost hope;
there is nothing to be saved –
so why fight so hard
to keep it afloat?

I cannot look into
your eyes anymore.
they are too cold –
too truthful;
the demise of us has
come to its climax.

yet, there is something
we share deep inside
that allows us to feel
one another's pain –
I want that to end too...

If it is truly over.    2001

# ONLY YOU

(THE REASON SHE COULDN'T PLAY BALL NO MORE)


I CAN'T WRITE WHAT I DON'T FEEL.

I WON'T SING WHAT DOESN'T HEAL.

I DON'T LIKE THAT I DON'T FEEL
FOR HIM WHAT I FELT FOR YOU;

I DON'T LIKE THAT I CAN'T SEAL
THE GIFT OF A GREAT LIFE
THAT OFFERS NOTHING BAD
WITH HIM

COMPARED TO THE HELL I HAD WHEN WITH YOU.

I CAN'T WRITE OF LOVE I DON'T FEEL –

A LOVE I'VE FELT FOR ONLY YOU

YET, MY HEART STILL TELLS
MY MIND HOW TO FEEL
THE WAY THAT I DO

AND I DO LOVE HIM;

I JUST CAN'T GET OVER YOU –

DAMN.

# I'M NO ZANE, BUT...

*I never knew what I wanted, until I looked into your eyes.*
*"Mine," he whispers.*
*"Yours," I breathe.*

*from <u>Fifty Shades of Grey</u>*

# The Perfect Orgasmic Cosmos
# (sheer masculinity)

I like it when it's erect
Standing tall with acceleration
Enjoying the suspense
Anticipating the moment
Until you totally emerge from within

You know what I mean

Even when it's a little laid to rest –
Finally – like an unagreeable issue
Blood-rushed and at attention
It can get back up with the slightest caress

You know what I mean

And especially when it's inside
Deeply tantalizing with excitement
Making the ride even better
Enhancing the overwhelming state of happiness
To gladly experience the gush of it all

You know what I mean

# a portrait of love

his thigh
over
her toe
under
her leg
wrapped in her arms
as they laid
there
together
his head rested
in the bosom
of her chest
his forehead
pressed by her hand
against
her breasts
close
near
her heart

# Dear Darling, my Ebony king,

Lay your head on my pillow.
Now, move it to the nipples of my breasts
>  So that I may feel you softly caress
>> Every nook, inch, and crevice –

Lay yourself on top of me
So that our bodies become one intertwining
>  And sexually unwinding
>  Getting ready for the slowly sensual grinding
>> Of you inside of me ooohhh baby!

Feel my juices flow
Every time that you go
>  Deeper and deeper into the realms of my soul
>  Where our two essences pour into one
>> Creating a whole
>> And blindly unfolding the story untold
>> That I truly do love you

As the sweat of your glistening wet body
Trickles from your nose to my belly button
>  All of a sudden –
>  I vibrate, shimmy, and shake
>> As your hands quickly stroke my back
>> Up and down and
>>> Up and again and
>>>> over again
>>> until I can bathe my face
>> into your ridged stomach muscles
>  carefully examining every move you make
cautiously awaiting all there is to take
>  of your spirit joined with mine
>  perfectly aligned
>>> with space, earth, and time

my complete sweetness,
chocolate treat
Pour that caramel all over me
>  So that I become free to taste you

And have you waste yourself on me
I and you totally completely in sync
And I now pledge myself
    Your dearest friend, lover, and mate

With lust-filled love always –
Signed,

Your Precious Mahogani

# did I like it...

when you caressed my essence with your
    journey-finder – pink, sleek, wet
        instrument of pleasure

when you took the plunge and
    went deep-sea diving to find my pearl,
        tickled it, and exploited my world

when you entered my curious walls
    and filled them with a passion so true-
        that let me know I was Your Boo

when you thrusted deeper inside
    when your eyes met with mine
        to unlock this thing that we now share

this guilt that I'm willing to bare
to see if there is none that can compare
to the lust in the glare of your stare
and I am completely aware
of your intentions (I think...)

did I like it?

Do bees pollinate flowers to assist in nature's growth?
Does the sun's light disperse the morning's glow?
Do animals in the spring birth life as we know?

at the sound of your voice,
    does my mind yell STOP when my body screams GO?!

did I like it...
can you tell...
that I did.

The thought that it could actually

Happen hovered about my mind, and

Even after getting here, I

Started to have cold feet. but

We are inevitable; can't deny it, tired of fighting it;

Ecstasy was our destination this day.

Egos were finally set aside.

Time to stop talking; our words became action – the

Eventual promises that

Spoke to our connected destinies and

Told our truth out loud.

Holding you, captivated by your frame

Anticipating your entrance

Never felt so natural, so real

Grinding my nails -

Our lovely lust - into existence over and over again

Very passionately pleasant with

Every stroke, motion, synchronized inhalation – I was

Right where I belonged for that moment in time… with You.

# through closed eyes

i took a bath
in lukewarm water
that turned burning
hot the second i felt
your hands caress my
legs spreading the
sweetly scented suds
over my breasts as my
back comfortably pressed
against your stern chest
and as my body began
to tingle from the wetness
of your lips
on my neck
in my ear
nibbling on my earlobes
i opened my eyes to find myself
alone in a tub
of cold, clear water
just reminiscing

# happy.Valentine's.date

hearts were racing
quick, fast pacing
as we were facing
looking into each other's eyes
like the brown was a surprise
or our distant demise

you walked up slow
my body said go
was this just a show
please, let me know
if this is real
exactly how you feel
do I acquire sex appeal

but like I said
before this flow is dead
you stepped to me
as humble as can be
it's your turn
what is the lesson to be learned
it's your move
what do you have to prove

let right here, right now
be the place –
you set the mood,
you set the pace
all I'll do is
bring the satin and the lace

# love poem no. 1

(inspired by the Love Jones soundtrack)

*I feel you*
    *beating on the drum*
        *of my heart*

*softly, slowly*
    *pounding a familiar*
        *rhythm of love*

*you take my hand,*
    *lead me to the floor,*
        *and embrace me*

*entice me*
    *with your fancy*
        *footwork and words*

*enchant me*
    *with your song*
        *of pleasant lust*

*strum the strings*
    *of that bass guitar*
        *digging deep, soul searching*

*you put me in*
    *an undeniable trance*
        *by your mere appearance*

*for, I feel you*
    *beating on the drum*
        *of my heart*

*softly, slowly*
    *pouring that familiar*
        *rhythm of love*

# A lover's confession

I thought
I heard you
whisper
whisper
soft, sweet
nothings in my ear
while you
took me
escorted me
to a place
I'd never been
before

I could have
sworn I saw
you smile
smile
lustfully at me
as you engaged in
drank the essence of
my sexual
fountain flowing free

I exhaled
fretfully
sighed
sighed
emotionally
motionlessly
caught in the
crossfire
of your love
open-mouthed
and close-eyed

I reached
for the crevice
creasing of
your back
allowing my hands
to rub
the manliness
that engulfed
my femininity

I searched
for a reasonable
conceivable
argument
for the way
I flinched
and twitched
when hearing
the new depth
of the bass
in your voice

I pondered
upon the
possibility
of this endless love
as I embraced you
engulfed you
became one with you
in one
strong
stroke
the same rhythm
that moved me
had been the music

we produced
together
last night

# i am downright angry – IN LOVE!

Never make someone your priority when you are only their option.

# based upon your decision,

i committed
an indecency
last night.
i had thoughts
about bedding
with another
make simply for
comfort and to
relieve my acute
loneliness –
just because
i could not
sleep with you.

why do you tell
me No so often
these days?
how can you deny me
the only body
i desire
to become one with?
is there
someone else
to hold you
those nights
you leave me cold
and alone
in my bed?

you'll never
understand
the difference
a comforted night
can make
or the joy it brings

in the morning.
waking up on
the wrong side
of the bed –
No, thank you;

i'd rather find
my comfort
in the arms of
someone else
and have a great day,
not wanting you
to be
my sunshine
in the morning.
please don't be upset!
it was you
who denied me
something as simple
as your small arms and
unmuscular
frame -

so i found
comfort in the
firm arms
and
washboard
stomach
of an
'untouchable'…
woke up to a
relentlessly
tantalizing
smile,

stood my ground,
caught my composure,
Then
called you
to say
Good Morning.


2001

# To The Young Man Who cried 'love'

I can't believe
    the words that come
    out of your mouth therefore
I can't trust you
    Anymore
Yet, I still love you
    but can't stand
    to be around you
The constant notion
of honesty rests solely
on my judgment
    but it is all a blur
You said I love you
    in vain
    before finally admitting
    the truth
Now, all the lies
you have lived through
are gone
And
So am I…
Cried wolf too many times
for me to believe
that you ever loved me
Even after last night
Even after this morning

01.20.00

# Sweet Dreams and Beautiful Cake

How is it that the inevitable became the unexpected?
Was it not what you had foreseen on your vivid imagination's screen?

Those scenes that awakened you out of your dreams
     With a smile on your face
Those same images that invaded my reveries
     causing me sleepless space

Why is it that my instincts were warning signals against you?
I know your kind; I should have run.
I should have resisted the urge for an intelligible fun
     Not realizing, not recognizing
     The game could never be won
     By me for I am only a pawn,

A façade – a translucent layer of your cake
And I hear your appetite for chocolate-flavored slices
     Isn't as immense as your taste for vanilla fudge
So let me turn my oven off now
Because I don't want to get burned!

# A THOUGHT TO KILL

CLOSE YOUR EYES…

IMAGINE:

CLOSE FRIENDS
FROM THE SAME AREA
NEVER MEETING EACH OTHER
UNTIL NOW
SHARING SOME COMMON BOND
UNFATHOMED

IN PUBLIC
WALKING SIDE BY SIDE
NEVER HAND IN HAND
HAVING THE SAME THOUGHTS
FINISHING EACH OTHER'S SENTENCES
INTIMATE CONVERSATIONS
OF PAST LOVES
AND RELATIONSHIPS
LAUGHING AT INSIDE JOKES
BETWEEN THE TWO
SMILES ONLY GIVEN TO EACH OTHER
WHISPERING SECRETS
ON THE COUCH PRIVATELY
IN THE DARK
THAT NO ONE ELSE
SHOULD KNOW

WHEN TROUBLES STRIKE
EVEN IN THE MIDDLE OF THE NIGHT
HE'S ALWAYS BEEN THERE
TO COMFORT HER
BY HER SIDE, TO HER AID
DESPITE THE COST
THE FRICTION AND TENSION

MOUNTING (AT HOME)
THE ADIMONSITY BUILDING (TOWARDS HER)

A LOVE BEING TESTED
A TRUST BEING BROKEN
WHILE THEIR FRIENDSHIP

INTENSIFIES

CAN YOU IMAGINE THAT?
CAN'T YOU SEE IT...

NOW,
BELIEVE THAT THEY ARE FUCKING!

# A THOUGHT REVISITED

(…OPENED MY EYES)

PRAY TELL ME WHY Y'ALL JUST NEVER HOOKED UP AGAIN? It's not even a friendship that Y'all have – it's a spiritual connection so (if y'all haven't already via the finding of the condom) why don't y'all just do everybody involved a favor and just do it! Y'all have built y'all's friendship up to that point. Y'all claim to be in love with other people but y'all make it difficult to be in a relationship with y'all. And once an emotional attachment is established, y'all be damned to let them walk away but maybe now is the time.

I guess I'm just jealous all over again so it's best I not be involved.

# caught on the flip side of funny

ain't it a trip that you just done flipped
because you think I've done wrong by you
ain't that some shit that you tried to commit
because you thought I was good for you
don't fake it – at ease, when you were aiming to please
but you couldn't stand at attention
why – pay it no mind because you thought I would find
another to replace you
and don't believe the hype 'cause I feel it's alright
that you never completely trusted me
or I you
it just goes to show exactly what kind of bastard you are –
one with mad double standards
for your kind is foul like a ball in left field
and you've unrightfully accused me because
you didn't know the deal
well, pay you no mind for it's over and done
oh boy, I must say, the rides were such fun!
but, this battle has just begun
so you don't believe me – that's cool, keep it real
but admit:
you are on the flipped side of funny
and the shit don't feel too wonderful at all, does it?
Bitch!

# phuck love –

(that shyt that's for the birds)

I'll settle for contentment
for happiness costs too much,
and my auntie taught me
to have expensive taste.

# Saved by the Bell!

This is no high school affair
    Because I know I never stared
Into any boy's eyes the way
    I looked into yours that day

This is no college escapade
    Or any rec room games I used to play
Because this is a pain
    I wish would go away

But there were so many stories,
    Too many lines;
Not enough truth
    And so many lies

Though I know you are not mine
    And I could never be yours
It still doesn't close this hole at my core
    Where you now reside
    Where sensibility and imagination collide
I yearn for a desired place to realign
    With you for just one moment in time

Yet, we are not speaking
I don't want to get accused of tweaking
And my defenses against you are frivolously weakening
    As your attention for me is slowly seeping
Through the cracks of lost lust
And tainted temptations

For it seems She has returned
Or maybe She never left…

# ...just like you...

I went out last night
while you stayed in
I saw a movie
(with *just a friend)*
while you slept restlessly
I danced, drank, and was merry
while you tossed and turned
I ate French fries and po-boys
while you dreamt of infidelity
I was held tight
when you awakened alone
I was being serenaded our favorite song
when I heard the phone ring
(and didn't answer it)
I was stargazing on the lake
when you paged me
(and I ignored it)
I was making love
when you started going crazy
I was creating a secret
but you already knew that
I wasn't going to tell you
I knew you were afraid to hear the truth
I didn't want to lie to you
You didn't want to hate me
so I told you what I wanted you to know
Angrily, you shrugged it off
like I usually do
because you finally realized
I followed your lead and
I did everything
just like you

2001

# i know it's in vain

but

i still
   think about
      dream of
         reminisce upon

the moments of
   pursuit
   persistence
   passion
   pain

i still
   desire to
      yearn for
         hope that
we can be
friends
when
it's all
said and
done

because
i apologize
and
i still
*heart

…the chaos
…the control
…the comfort
…the complacency

of not being able
to love freely

yet,
i miss that
and
i miss –
You

# I LIVE
# I LAUGHED
# I'VE LEARNED

How vain it is to sit down to write when you have not stood up to live.
-Henry David Thoreau

# Role Reversal

If dog is man's best friend, who is dog's best friend – a hydrant?

What if man is dog's best friend...don't men
    lay with other dogs and get fleas...
    chase after cats...
    scratch themselves all the time...
    'wag their tails' when they want to play...
    'bark' at enemies or signs of danger...
    smell their bitches when in heat...
    mark their territories...
    want affection and attention at the wrong times...

Are men simply two-legged dogs in disguise? (2000)

# No Pity Party Here!

Insecure in my position in his life –
not actually,
    no, not anymore
Insecure in your position in his
life – YES!

You see,
It's vulnerable bitches like you
(or having the potential thereof)
that makes us
good women sick –
because we see you
get rejected time
    and time again and
see you latch onto our men
claiming to be
just
a friend –

You see,
At one time –

We good ones
have ridden
    that lonely road
    too
    but
we learned,
preserved,
and became
stronger
so Love Yourself
and leave our men alone
in time,
if you are truly
deserving of one,
you'll
Receive
a man of your own –
but,
I
wouldn't
hold
my breath! (2001)

# Love Jones' Stories #3: Acceptance

"Love's rollercoaster from a mental cipher"

Okay, now I know we're friends and
we'll probably be that until the end
but we are confuse about our situation
yes – WE are confused;
don't deny it…don't reject this!
Can you accept this the way that it is?
I don't believe WE can!
I know I can't, I mean it's a bit much.
Okay, so maybe I'm attracted to you
And just maybe I like you a lot
And just maybe I would love to be your girl
But we're involved in this situation –
YOU KNOW WHAT I MEAN!
It's not a bad thing,
but it could be a better thing;
only if we both are ready.
Ready for what…
Okay, now you want to act like you don't know –
Ready for Us! To be together, as in a union –
without interferences
from ex realms and former worlds
that have haunted us for the last time;
only if you're ready
will We ever become one.
Am I ready?
Yes, I mean I think I am,
I thought that I knew that I was…
But what about our happy friendship?
Won't it be affected?
Will it grow and prosper like a syrupy sweet
or will it fester, rot, dry up, and die?
What the hell – but anyway-
The question that I ask is:
Are our worlds ready for Us?
(1999)

# Let's Wait Awhile

It's the bottom of the ninth inning as
    he steps up to the plate
        with his bat in his hand,
            his helmet strapped on tight.
As she awaits the hit,
    she thinks of how great it will be
        to cross home plate and
            score for the first time.
He swings and strikes;
    she sighs with anxiety.
        She wets the mound –
            A fast one's coming next;
He swings – tip, strike two.
    Now he is frustrated;
        he can't find his stroke.
            He rotates his bat in his hand,
            now ready for the next pitch.
She looks into his eyes
    faintly as if she's ready to die.
She pitches the ball,
    closes her eyes,
        And HOME RUN!
She screams with pleasure
    As he steadily rounds the bases
    Trying to withstand his excitement…
But as he rounds third,

He loses his helmet;
      He doesn't stop to put it back on.
His pace quickens as he strides over
    home plate and into the dugout.
She follows him into the dugout,
    but he's not there.
She calls for his signal,
    but there's no response.
Coach comes in to relay the painful message to her:
    I am afraid I have some bad news for you.
    No more pitching for you for a while…
She holds her head in her hands
    And leaves Coach's office.

Some time passes - it's the World Series –
She pitches one last game alone
    for nine of the longest hours of her life
    to deliver a game winning pitch,
All because she didn't anticipate
    This possible result to the event
        She had waited all of her sixteen years to accomplish…

And now it's all changed forever.

# special delivery

I will kick a nigguh's ass
If my monthly flight doesn't pass
And it will be all hell
If internally I don't feel well
For if tomorrow I should die
Keep my cipher rolling high
Until then I have plans to beat
A nigguh's ass for phuckin' over me!

# don't make me over

I AM

... a product of your irresponsibility
... the Frankenstein you created
... your worst nightmare and greatest fantasy
... not what you wanted me to become
... what you wished I hadn't learned
... your hatred and abuse
... the forbidden fruit you should not desire
... a life should not try to relive
... the grace that amazed you
... the sun that once shone a little brighter
... the key that unlocked opportunity
... the time you want to turn back
... that mistake you badly want to correct
... some advice you should have kept
... a product of your undying, forgotten love

# i don't even know how i got here...

this pain –
    a result of a yearning
    to hear your voice
    to see your face
    to feel your touch

this is crazy

i don't even know how i got here…

mad at my actions
confused by my thoughts
stifled by this connection
that was once a 2-way street
now,
a dead end

i don't even know how i got here…

writing these feelings
    that i can't explain
    that i won't vocalize
    that should have never become a reality
again

i don't even know how i got here or
where i'm going
and it scares me
shitless

# Can I Talk?

Had I known
Of the details –
those intricate
aspects of your
broken love and
battered life –
I guess I would
have been a lot
less selfish
I would have
listened more
attentively to
your lonely thoughts
knew that it wasn't
your ego that
boasted but
your heart
that yearned
to be healed
that it wasn't
A game but your
Defense mechanisms
Kicking in
To shield you
From further hurt
But do remember
That shutting down,
The façade,
The constant flirtations
Mean that
You're giving up
And you are not a quitter
You are a fighter
You are a lover
And you are loved

Stop faulting yourself
For things you can't
Control
Stop making excuses
For the lack of trust
Lack of intimacy
The overabundance of
Family interventions
Even when you don't
Want them to intervene
Furthering the rift
It's frustrating
I know
But don't give up
Stand up and
Fight for the love
You have for her
Prove it to her
That she is the one
Your one and only
Lifelong love
Put your second guesses aside
And cast out
Her extra baggage
That is weighing
Your relationship down
If it is truly
What you desire for your life
I applaud your efforts
To be true although
There are several obstacles
Blocking your progress
Don't let them take your joy
Don't let her steal your heart
Don't let me cloud your mind

I now understand
Who I am
Who I was
What I was supposed to be
Since I finally have
That choice to make
For myself
Since I finally know
The truth
All I can say is
*Je suis tres desole',*
*mon ami*
Truly I am.
I'm sorry
That you've been
Harboring
Hiding
Hurting-
In time,
I hope that
Forgiveness
can be
The foundation
Of our friendship.
I pray that
You forgive
Them,
Her, and
Me...
And find your way
Back to life
And to love.

# Full-time Man

I need a full time man,
not a part-time lover
or a fair weather friend
whose love is undercover.

I need a full time man –
tall, dark, handsome, and smart,
not someone who resembles a frog
and has a personality
the size of a wart.

I need a full time man,
not one of those street rats
who, when trouble comes, runs
as fast as he can turn his back.

I need a full time man,
not seasonal maintainer
or a female entertainer
whose priorities aren't stable.

I need a full time man;
I don't want no cheap thrill
who steps with some corny lines –
that *ish*, you can definitely chill.

I need a full time man –
someone with their mind in focus
able to care for me who won't
pull no tricks, no magic,
no hocus pocus!

I need a full time man:
a true brother who will be my friend,
my protector, but all lover;
and together the adventures of life,
we can discover.

I need a full time man…

round the clock on the dot
always there when I need
a helping hand
maybe cooks and cleans
but definitely understands
as sharp as new double breasted suit
works hard every day to
bring home the loot
wines me and dines me so elegantly
softly caresses my tensely
anxious body
fulfills me and thrills me
sexually and mentally
never quick to judge me but
believes, trusts, and learns of me
doesn't try to control me, but
rather consoles me

You see, that's what I need –
A full time man!

# After-Math

Do you believe in life after love or love before life?
After lust even is a concept worth conceiving;

Can you accept the silver lining of the cloud
After the storm has washed away all possibility?

How do you look a broken mirror in its face
After the bad luck has been inflicted upon the reflection?

Why does the grass plain in Spain flood immensely
After a slight sprinkle of disarranged rain?

How come and why does or how did because what was
Where it was when it was bound to happen.

After the lust, the storm,
        the bad luck, and the rain -

I completely lost my train of thought,
lost control of my mind,
subsequently losing control of my life

After shit happened.

# Alcohols Synonymous: Ode to Liquor

drink Gin and sin
    and dance and die
sip Crown, fall down
    and eat and sigh
V.O. – too slow
    then smoke, too high
J.B. with tea
    laugh loud and lie
Vodka gotcha
    gone now, sexed guy
Hennessey, have mercy on me
    up, up to the sky
Amaretto gotta go
    to the liquor store close by
one Tequila,
    two Tequila…
        three Tequila –

        Floor!

# My Self Found Serenity

*Hell hath no fury that Heaven cannot conquer. There is no greater fury in a man's life than a woman scorned. I'm glad I'm no longer that woman. Let life's love rule; above else, never forgetting to be true to yourself because in the end, you're all that really matters. This is my prayer in Jesus's name.*

*Amen.*
*4.30.02*

# Sacrificed

Souls mated by the locking of lips
Spirits aligned by the locking of time
Love ended by the locking of heart

# welcome your soulmate

how is it that the only person
    that can dry your tears is
the same person that made you
    cry them in the first place?

have you ever been so cold that
    Hell's fiery flames only defrost you;
been so hot that below zero
    feels like 110° in the shade?

has your being ever experienced
    such a loneliness that meditation
through music only increases
    the pain?

have you ever been in love so much
that it hurts...

# freedom

i refuse to wait for my turn
to get messed over
once again
so excuse me if i am not
obliged to carry out your agenda


(2000, rev 2015)

# The promised sacrifices of ifs

If I could count
the many lost loves
or should have beens
in my life,
I would rather endure
the pain all again;
because it would be far
too long before I felt a love
like this one-
so before this becomes
a distant has been,
another statistic
in my record book
of failed relationships,
I need to know:
is my loving you in vain?
do you feel this
the way I do or
just scared to admit the truth;
that this thing is
beyond me and you.
if I would tell
the many stories of
disillusions and denial-
the could have beens
in my life,

I would fall asleep
and dream of you…
being with you openly,
reciprocated feelings
for once with no other
interferences
and straight-up honesty.
I want you
to know how I feel
if already you don't.
I want to know
how you feel,
exactly what you want.
If I could recount
the tales of love
desired, and died tonight,
I would rest in the thoughts
of endless pleasures
and unknowingness that
tickle my emotions,
allowing this thing –
our love to be free.
But these are only ifs…
(2000)

# My Self Controls Itself

*My world – it moves so fast today;*
*The past – it doesn't seem to be going away fast enough*
*and life is testing me every hour of every day.*
*Those who need to cry for me only*
*scream out in pain – a feeble attempt to get attention*
*or spark an argument, not knowing which way to turn.*
*I'm tired of trying to be what others*
*want of me because it's sheer unhappiness.*
*I hate living here in this negativity!*
*I'm tired of being an outcast.*
*I'm fed up with getting treated like a child -*
*tired of being ridiculed for others' faults.*
*But I would like some peace in my life,*
*in my mind, in my heart, and in my soul.*
*This is my prayer in Jesus' name.*

*Amen.*
*06.05.02*

# game is just

idle thoughts and
    complex mentalities
brief memories and
    lustful cries
heartbroken pains and
    tearful sighs
game is just
rendered and
    unknowingly played

# AFTER SHOCKS

SIMPLE SPACE HOLDING TIME
ENDLESS WHILE EVOKING
UNREQUITTED LOVE AS THE MIND
SCRIPTS STORIES –
MERE STATEMENTS OF LIFE

# no doubt: abusive behaviors

i want to see you
i want to see you
    like i want to meet
Jesus when i die
i want to rape your mind
    with my eyes
    and make your thoughts hurt
make your psyche shiver
    by the touch of my vibe
pulsations of positive energy
overwhelming the past negativity
i want to beat you
    unconsciously
    with the changes that
    have occurred within me
i want to blacken your eyes
    blind you with my new
    sense of self
i want to pin you down
    to the floor and
forcefully feed you my love
    through intravenous tubes
    to sustain life
i want the desires of your heart
    the contents of your once open
soul
i want to feel the essence
    of the chocolate that
    made me melt
    inside of my walls again
i want to regain that
cosmic connection that alluded time
    to stand steadfast
(but stagnant)
i, i just –

i just want to
    breathe you
    and get high again
i just want to stop loving you like
this, yo!
until then
i just want to see you
    even if it's with her
    by your side
the constant reminder
    of the way
I should have been

# I Am A Poet.

Poetry only has one goal –
of rediscovering and uncovering language.

Chandler Todd Fritz

A CONCRETE POEM takes the shape of an object in the poem or simply forms a shape in which the format of the poem is a CONCRETE structure on paper. Can you see the shape of this poem?

A Flower and a Vase
Wednesday,
while sitting
reading the
Literary Art of
An Intellectual,
I watched
Immortality
be conceived;
probably something
as simple as an assignment
instructed by some futile
Mortal – evolved into a masterpiece
of Permanence; shapes, lines,
shades, colors – engraved by the
hand of a mere human; it would be
so pleasant to smell the petals of its
Eternity as they drape the
side of its base. Thursday,
everyone beheld its
Authenticity
several times over –
(from different perspectives)
Still, truly Art.

# When is the end?

We live in this mean world **everyday**
Awaiting the potency of time's **delay**;
And all the love we share with **others**
Brings us closer to a world stronger than **brothers**;
Yet, the world revolves around, saves the **day**,
and life parades on in its great **masquerade**.

*Features end rhyme and yields itself to a specific rhyme scheme (A A B B A A)*

# we hate Love

the Entity that
desires everyone.

it sneaks in. it
turns friends.

it hurts bad. it
sings sad.

it hits hard. it
awes guard.

it stings, warns. it
leaves scorned.

it gives life. It
adds strife.

it laughs loud. it
smiles proud.

it gets sweet. it
grows deep.


...the previous poem is based upon Gwendolyn Brooks' "we real cool." The rhythm of the poem helps the lines of staccato march on the page and set the tone. Word choice has to be specific in order to achieve the poem's message about love's rollercoaster ride of disguise, demise, and deepening.

# Prom Night Eve

Mirror, mirror in my room
Show me now – my currency doomed;
For an imperfection has slapped itself
upon my frontal canvas!

Even though this is a very short poem, it has a very distinct **tone**: the emotion you hear through the use of specific **word choice**. The tone is frantic, anxious; it's Prom Night Eve and the narrator has just realized she has a zit – what kind of **mood** would that put you in?! The word slapped conveys that it seemed deliberate; her currency (current situation) is doomed, exhibiting a quite negative **connotation**. What teenager do you know is actually elated about a pimple showing up on their face the night before Prom?!!!

# The Nocturnal Id

scattered dreams
jumping from scene to scene
through the subconscious crypts
of the mind
where life is erased                                                    5

into

stratospheres
of one's fears led by
the un-reality of
suppressed thoughts                                                     10
smeared onto the walls of time

through

stagnant tombs
and broken-hearted wombs
fretfully crossed by                                                    15
Reason –
to dance with night's closed-minded

soon


This poem features a few elements of figurative language: <u>personification</u> – giving human attributes to inanimate objects (lines 16-17); <u>assonance</u> – the repetition of vowels sounds within a line of poetry (line 17); end rhyme – rhyming patterns at the end of lines of poetry; and imagery – images appealing to one or more of the five senses. There are elements and features of this poem which would classify its structure as free verse (the stanzas are not standard, lacks correct usage of punctuation and capitalization) and traditional (there is a distinctive rhythm presented and use of end rhyme).

# love for you

i
i remember
i remember when
i remember when
    i planted this seed -
i watered it every day.
i waited
i wondered
    and wandered
but watered…
It never grew.

FEATURED ELEMENT: REPETITION – what is the significance of the repeated words in this poem?

# The Women of Indigo Place

Whatever happened to
the three little monkeys that
bumped their heads
while jumping
in and out of his bed?

One took the spoon,
met up with the cow,
and jumped over the moon.

One jumped into the shoe -
now lonely, sad, and blue
to play games of birth with Mother Goose.

The other one jumped onto
the turnip truck, fucked up her luck,
and died!

No more monkeys jumping in and out of his bed.

This poem alludes to the nursery rhyme, "3 Little Monkeys" and incorporates an **extended metaphor** comparing the three females to the monkeys 'that were jumping [in and out of his] bed'. **Allusions** are references made to other pieces of literature, songs, people, events, news etc. as they have occurred in the world (similar to the old comprehension strategy of making connections - whether the connection be text to self, to world, or to text). The following poem alludes to various popular, R&B songs while the speaker communicates an expression of positive feelings for someone.

# music head

you got me going half-crazy
you – this complicated melody
that got me wishing I
could die without you
because I'm ready for love
and you're all the man I need
and all I need to get by and
it's taken way longer than a day
to recognize you as my sunshine
but you know
time waits for no one so
while I was talking that long walk
thinking of the way you love me
Bay bah
I figured out that
the way love goes and
you knowing that
I love you
became the bittersweet memory of
a foolish, silly bitch in love
and now I'm all cried out
and you've spread your
wings and began to fly

and I'm still feenin',
weak because the one I
gave my heart to
walked out of my life –
have you ever loved someone
so much it made you cry?
how does it feel?
can we talk?
how come you don't
call me anymore?
anyway,
I wanted to be your sweet lady,
feel your whip appeal all night;
then again, no no no no -
I'm just bitter;
you made a fool of me
yet, I await better days…
I'll tell you how I feel about
you night and day.
you will appreciate this
woman's work;
are you looking forward to tonight's
red light special…
let me break it down - sshhhhhhhh
you might not always be
there when I call,
but you're always on time!

In this poem, various R&B song titles are used to convey the message of the
poem.

# Love Jones' Stories #11: Stagnation

I chased a dream
to the end of a rainbow
frantically running
to find a pot of coal
left there by a despondent
leprechaun who accused
me of wanting a fantasy
to become a reality
while it was still raining;
the truth still a mystery
for it was consumed into
a nightmare's fog and
hidden deep within the belly
of a child;
the product of his hatred
because the sun didn't shine
bright enough for him
to see that the light
had never been dimmed
on the greener side
of the fence
so the rainbow only reflects
black, grey, and
an unpeaceful shade of white
now…
so I stand still
in the midst of the storm
waiting for this jones
to finally come down
and slap me with
a fresh breeze of reality.

FEATURED ELEMENT(S)

IRONY: the expression of one's meaning by using language that normally signifies the opposite, typically for humorous or emphatic effect

OXYMORON: a figure of speech in which apparently contradictory terms appear in conjunction

The following poem features a hint of **imagery** as a few of the images appeal to the reader's sight, hearing, taste, touch, and feeling (tangible or emotional). It can also be categorized as **free verse** since it lacks conventional stanza structure and does not contain rhyme or a specific rhythm. (*M'enerve* is French for *that annoys me.*) Also featured in this poem is an example of **homonyms/homophones**: words that sound very similar in speech, but contain different spellings and have very distinctly, different denotations.

# William M'Enerve (1998)

While walking through the halls on my way to enhance my knowledge of Britain's greatest composer of written, unsung songs of gallant men and chivalry, I fell asleep. Drained of energy and my desire to learn, I sat <u>idle</u> as the rouge coifed, scruffy-faced figure called professor dragged on and on, sarcastically rambling about an issue uncared about. Drifting in and out of consciousness, I found myself rapidly losing respect for this shit forced upon my brain because it is suggested by a group of educationally advanced pricks that I acquire facts about this possible homosexual. No disrespect to this exalted, <u>idol</u> god of literature, I just don't want to be here right now!

# 5 steps before being with you again

*I looked into your eyes and*
*I wanted to die because*
*in your eyes, I saw*
*your despair, your defeat*

*I listened to your voice*
*and wished I was deaf*
*because I heard the cries*
*of your broken heart*

*I smelled the aroma of your cologne*
*and my nose shriveled up*
*because I beheld the scent*
*of your favorable displeasure*

*I tasted the essence*
*of your forbidden soul*
*and I shrieked loudly-*
*your taste buds soured on me*

*I felt the pain of your body*
*and my sympathies were with you*
*because I wanted to console*
*the absence of your presence*

*but I couldn't because*
*my heart, my being, my soul -*
*shattered into condemned pieces*
*smothered in wrenching pain -*
*wouldn't allow me to help you*
*because you caused all of this*

*Again.*

1998
The featured poetic device is imagery.

This poem is derived from the **Shakespearean sonnet** format. Take notice of the rhyme scheme featured in the first stanza and the ending couplet (even though it does not rhyme).

# So I Twisted His Sonnet

…they say two wrongs don't make it right,
but two negatives equal one positive.
So why did we always fuss and fight
because we never made up completely happy.
And how many storms will pour down tonight
before the calm of the silver lining shines through;

If something so powerful (like Love) can blind your sight,
then learn to love the one that loves you back.

# Trapeze, Trampolines, & Transitions

Know no limits in life is what I used to think and
the sky isn't necessarily your limit so don't you blink;
For you'll miss out on your chance at success and
your grand disappointment will be all there is to profess.

My cipher keeps rolling like the world continues to turn
and all of the negativity hindering my path has to be burned;
For I have embarked upon a new journey, a quest for a productive life
that has no room for struggle, obstacles, or strife.

There is a Higher Power that helps me disarrange my flaws –
He aids, nurtures, and guides me in eliminating the effects of life's raw cause;
and even if I fail, I know some truth will be the prelude...
*It's not my aptitude, but my attitude that determines my altitude*

How high can you fly?
1998

FEATURED ELEMENTS: alliteration (in the title, there is the repetition
of the tr- consonant cluster at the beginning of the words; by definition,
alliteration is the repetition of consonant sounds at the beginning of words
within a line of poetry), end and internal (rhyming within a line of poetry)
rhyme, allusion (the last line is a quote credited to James Caan, a motivational
speaker)

The following poem contains a **refrain** – just like the chorus of a song, it is repeated (with little modification) for emphasis (SEE the 2nd and 4th stanzas). Also, notice the definite rhythm of this poem: it is jazzy, sultry; there is a change in **tone** (the feelings evoked to the reader) by the end of the poem. Sometimes, there is a distinct difference between mood and tone; sometimes, the comprehension of these terms is interchangeable.

## incognita

draped in sheets of mahogany
dipped into the consciousness of morality
created in the inevitable shadows of a prophetic end

she walks with danger
her head held high
she dances an upbeat second line
    to get by

hidden emotions trapped in time
distorted memories consumed with a tampered mind
her life: a soap opera to be showcased
    through her rhymes

she danced with danger
her head held nigh
she flirts with illusions
as her sorrows, she hides

# freestyle

i can't write
angry
screaming
rebellious poems
for the politicians
who think
we don't
have a clue
i won't write
another sad
loss of love poem
for the lonely
brokenhearted
lovesick soul
waiting for it
to happen
again
i don't write
rhyme
all the time
for those who want
to feel the
rhythm
of the meaning
through the words
while they hit
their hands
to their legs
to find the beat
(shit,
that's what music does;
i never claimed
to be a musician)
i wanna hit
you with

that hee: hee, hee
hee, hee yeah
mixed with
a little
woo-ha
flavor
in your ear
things that make
you say
damn,
that's tight –
so fresh and
so clean
wondering
who is that
mad lyricist?
how she flow so good!
i want to
get into your mind
pull out the
negative
replace it with
some positive
innovative
renovated
illuminated
sky written
messages
you can tell
your friends
and if, when
i write a poem
that does this,
then am I
truly able to be labeled

as a
Poet
and can proclaim
myself to be a poetess:
a female
who can steal
some others' life
dealt hand and
make it original enough
to accept it as
her own
and
her being real.

Printed in the United States
By Bookmasters